Record Of A Creative CEO

Master Plan, Challenges, Success.

By

Larry M. White

Record of a creative ceo.

Copyright © 2023 by Larry M. White.

Record of a creative ceo.

Table Of Contents

Introduction

The position of CEO is both challenging and thrilling in the fast-paced world of corporate leadership, where decisions can influence entire industries and millions of lives.

In addition to going beyond board meetings and quarterly reports, this diary provides a fascinating look into the daily activities of a CEO. It explores the personal and professional journey of a person tasked with guiding the ship of a sizable corporation.

Getting to the Corner Office: the Journey.

The journey to the corner office is more than just a career move; it's a transformational journey filled with highs and lows, successes and failures.

We'll look at the route that got us to the executive suite in this chapter.

We'll reveal the steps taken to rise to the top of the corporate ladder, from the early years of education and internships to the critical moments that defined leadership skills.

Why Maintain a CEO Journal?

In the world of corporate goliaths, keeping a CEO diary may seem unorthodox.

The motivations for this practice, however, are explained in this chapter. CEOs gain a useful tool for self-reflection, learning, and mentoring by writing down their ideas, difficulties, and insights.

We'll look at the concrete advantages and the part a diary plays in influencing leadership, judgment, and personal development.

You'll learn the importance of this diary in preserving leadership lessons for future generations through these pages.

Chapter 1

A CEO's Day in the Life.

The daily perspectives of a CEO can change depending on the sector, the size of the company, and the particular difficulties they encounter.
But the typical activities of a CEO are as follows:

1 Meeting: CEOs frequently have a full schedule of meetings.
The executive team, department heads, investors, clients, and external stakeholders are all included in these meetings. These meetings can discuss anything from strategy discussions to financial performance.

2 Making Decisions: CEOs frequently have to decide on important matters that could have a significant effect on the business.
These choices could pertain to capital expenditures, market expansion, product development, and more.

3 Strategy Development: CEOs are essential in determining the long-term strategy of the business. They help the organization set goals, spot growth opportunities and coordinate efforts to meet these targets.

4 Crisis management: Unexpected difficulties and crises are a part of every job.

Whether a crisis is brought on by erratic market conditions, public relations difficulties, legal difficulties, or internal conflicts, CEOs must be equipped to handle it.

5 Communication: The CEO is frequently the public face of the business. They communicate in a variety of ways, including internally with their staff and externally with the press, shareholders, and the general public.

6 Networking: It's essential to establish and maintain connections with associates in the field, partners, and potential investors.

To strengthen these relationships, CEOs may go to conferences, business gatherings, and networking dinners.

7 Employee Engagement: A constant concern is making sure that employees are inspired to work hard and are in line with the company's vision.

Through town hall meetings, feedback sessions, and recognition initiatives, CEOs can interact with their staff.

8 Financial Oversight: CEOs keep a close eye on the business's financial situation.

To make sure the business is on track to meet its financial objectives, this entails reviewing financial reports, budgets, and forecasts.

9 Innovation and Adaptation: CEOs must keep up with business developments and technological advances.

For the company to remain competitive, it must promote an innovation-friendly culture.

10 Innovation and adaptability: CEOs must keep up with business developments and technological advances.

For the company to remain competitive, it must promote an innovation-friendly culture.

11 Personal Time Management: Juggling a demanding work schedule with a personal life is a significant challenge.
To make sure they have time for their families, hobbies, and relaxation, CEOs frequently develop time management strategies.

It's critical to remember that a CEO's day can be extremely dynamic, and they must be adaptable and flexible to respond to shifting conditions and priorities.
As a company develops and the business environment changes, the specific insights and difficulties a CEO faces might also change over time.

Balancing Act: Work, Family, And Health

As a CEO, juggling work, family, and health can be difficult, but it's crucial for long-term success and well-being. Here are some tactics to help you strike that balance:

Set self-care as a top priority.

Plan regular times for exercise, rest, and leisure.

Stay hydrated and follow a healthy diet.

Make time for your interests and favorite pursuits.

Set Limits:

Your work hours should be precisely stated and adhered to.

Give your team tasks to complete, and put your trust in them to handle accountability.

To avoid overcommitting, get better at saying no when it's necessary.

Time management.

Prioritize tasks by using time management strategies like the Eisenhower Matrix. Restrict meetings and make use of effective communication channels.

To minimize context switching, group related tasks together.

Family time is good.

Plan family activities and make spending time with loved ones a priority.

Share your work commitments with your family and involve them in the planning process.

Delegate and give power to:

Trust your team to manage daily operations.

If you want to make sure that your team is prepared to take on more responsibility, invest in leadership development.

Make Good Use of Technology.

Utilize technology to communicate and work remotely to cut down on commute time.

The use of work-related technology during family and personal time should be constrained.

Look for Support:

To get expert advice and help manage stress, think about hiring a coach or therapist.

Join forces with CEOs or mentors who have a track record of balancing work and life.

Establish priorities and a plan.

Make time for work, family, and self-care in a realistic weekly or monthly schedule.

Always evaluate your priorities and make changes as necessary to reflect your current situation.

Acquire the ability to disconnect.
Make it a habit to take time off from work, especially on holidays or other days off.
To control expectations when you are unavailable, use out-of-office notifications.
Keep Your Health.
Keep an eye on your mental and physical health regularly. Don't ignore signs of stress or burnout; get help if necessary.
Keep in mind that finding a work-life balance is a process that requires ongoing adjustment as circumstances change.
To succeed and be happy as a CEO over the long term, it is crucial to put your health and family's needs before your work obligations.

Leadership And Strategy

Undoubtedly, a successful organization's CEO must possess both leadership and strategy. CEOs typically offer their companies vision, direction, and general leadership.

They are in charge of establishing the company's long-term success and making important decisions.

To be effective, a leader and a plan must:

1. Vision: A CEO should have a distinct vision for the future of the business and effectively convey this vision to stakeholders and employees.

2. Develop and put into action a well-thought-out plan known as strategic planning to meet the goals and objectives of the business.

3. Making important decisions that are in line with the company's vision and strategy, which frequently involves analyzing risks and opportunities.

4. Establishing a solid leadership team and a supportive workplace culture through team building.

5. Ability to adjust the strategy as necessary in response to shifting market conditions.

6. To ensure alignment with the company's goals, communication must be effective with all parties involved, including customers, investors, and employees.

7. Accountability: Being held responsible for results, both by oneself and by the leadership group.

These factors are combined by effective CEOs to guide their companies toward expansion and profitability.

Please feel free to ask if you need any clarification or more information on any of these points.

Chapter 2.

Deciding Difficult Matters.

A key responsibility of a CEO is the ability to make difficult choices. CEOs frequently have to make difficult decisions with serious consequences for their companies. Here are some fundamental guidelines that CEOs frequently adhere to when making difficult choices:

1. **Data-Driven Decision-Making:** CEOs base their decisions on data and analysis. They gather pertinent data, evaluate risks, and take into account possible outcomes.

2. **Unambiguous Vision and Strategy:** Decisions should be in line with the company's long-term Vision and Strategic Objectives. This makes it more likely that difficult decisions will benefit the organization as a whole.

3. CEOs must take into account the interests of a variety of stakeholders, including clients, investors, and the general public.

4. Ethics: It's crucial to uphold moral principles. Making difficult decisions requires integrity, adhering to rules of conduct, and following the law.

5. CEOs frequently have to make unpopular decisions, which requires courage and conviction. People must have the courage to stand by their decisions and articulate them clearly.

6. Planning for contingencies can help to reduce the risks associated with making difficult decisions. Planning for various scenarios and having contingency plans in place.

7. To get multiple viewpoints before making a decision, CEOs may consult with their leadership group, board of directors, or trusted advisors.

8. To ensure transparency and buy-in from stakeholders, it is crucial to communicate the motivations behind difficult decisions as well as their anticipated effects.

9. CEOs are aware that not every choice will be ideal, and they learn from their mistakes.
They take lessons from their errors and change course as necessary.

Depending on their leadership style and the unique circumstances of their organization, each CEO may take a different approach to making difficult decisions.
Please feel free to provide more information if you have a specific scenario or query about a CEO's difficult decision-making so that I can provide more specialized insights.

Creating And Managing High-Performance Teams

A CEO's crucial responsibility is to create and manage high-performance teams. An organization's success is frequently built on its effective teams. When creating and managing high-performance teams, CEOs should take into account the following major strategies and principles.

1. CEOs should take a proactive role in attracting and hiring top talent.

Finding people who share the company's values and have the necessary training and experience is crucial.

2. To give the team direction and motivation, it is important to clearly define the team's goals and to articulate the team's vision.

3. Trusting team members to take charge of their actions and make decisions promotes a sense of accountability and responsibility.

4. Diversity and inclusion: Creating diverse teams with a variety of backgrounds and viewpoints can result in more innovative problem-solving.

5. Effective Communication: Team members and the CEO must communicate openly and honestly. Feedback and updates regularly help to maintain alignment.

6. Leadership Development: Team members can benefit from investing in leadership development programs, which can be used to develop future leaders and boost productivity.

7. Recognizing and rewarding team members for their contributions and accomplishments can increase motivation and morale.

8. Resolution of Conflicts: A positive work environment must be maintained by promptly and constructively resolving conflicts within the team.

9. Encourage a culture of continuous learning and improvement to help teams adapt to shifting conditions and maintain competitiveness.

10. Leading by Example: CEOs should model their own conduct and work ethics for the company. Leading by example motivates groups to deliver their best work.

11. Invest in Team Building: Participating in team-building exercises on occasion can enhance the level of trust and cooperation between team members.

12. Teams with high performance are results-oriented. CEOs should set performance benchmarks and hold their teams accountable for meeting them.

It's important to keep in mind that developing and managing high-performance teams is a continuous process that calls for commitment and focus.

CEOs should customize their strategy to fit the unique needs and objectives of each organization and team.

Chapter 3

Lessons Learned From Managing Crises.

Any CEO must be adept at crisis management, and CEOs can gain important insights from handling crises.

The following are some salient lessons that CEOs frequently draw from their involvement in crisis management.

1. Being proactive and having a well-thought-out crisis management plan in place before a crisis arises is essential.

Roles, duties, and communication techniques should all be outlined in this plan.

2. Effective Communication: In times of crisis, timely and clear communication is crucial.

CEOs are taught the value of communicating with stakeholders and promptly resolving their issues.

3. Being flexible and adaptable in their approach is essential for CEOs as crises are frequently unpredictable. They gain the ability to act swiftly in situations that are constantly changing.

4. Cohesive leadership teams are essential for crisis management. CEOs are aware of the value of unity, cooperation, and trust among their top executives.

5. Transparency: In times of crisis, honesty and open communication foster trust. CEOs are aware that withholding information or downplaying the seriousness of a situation can have unfavorable long-term effects.

6. The welfare and safety of workers, clients, and other stakeholders must come first. CEOs discover that people should come first.

7. Learn from Mistakes: Every crisis presents a chance for growth and learning. CEOs should conduct post-crisis analyses to determine what went wrong and how to avoid similar problems in the future.

8. In times of crisis, CEOs become skilled at effectively allocating resources, including cash, people, and technology.

9. CEOs frequently use a scenario-based approach to prepare for different types of crises.
When unplanned events happen, they can react more quickly as a result.

10. Maintaining good relations with significant stakeholders, including regulators, investors, and the media, is essential for controlling the effects of a crisis.

11. Long-Term Thinking: CEOs understand that, in addition to dealing with the current crisis, they also need to think about how it will affect the organization's reputation in the long run.

12. Resilience: Successfully navigating crises can strengthen an organization's and its CEO's resiliency in the face of upcoming difficulties.

CEOs frequently reflect on their prior experiences to better anticipate and handle upcoming crises because crisis management is an ongoing learning process.

Effective crisis management strategies frequently emphasize being proactive, maintaining transparency, and placing stakeholder welfare first.

Market Uncertainty.

CEOs frequently have to deal with market volatility, which calls for a strategic and flexible approach.

Here are some key strategies for CEOs dealing with market turbulence:

1 Continued Vigilance: Keep an eye out for changes in consumer preferences, market trends, and the state of your sector.

To make wise decisions, you must have access to current information.

2. Scenario Planning: Create various plans of action, including worst-case scenarios, for various market conditions. This aids in preparing you for unanticipated turbulence.

3. Understand the requirements and preferences of your customers.

Customer opinions and loyalty are invaluable in trying times.

4. Cost management: Analyze and improve the cost structure of your business.

Find opportunities for cost savings or increased efficiency that won't affect the level of service or the satisfaction of the customer.

5. Foster an agile organizational culture.

Encourage staff to be open to new concepts and innovations and to adjust to changing market dynamics quickly.

6. To spread risk, think about diversifying your product or service offerings or entering new markets.

7. Maintain a solid financial position with plenty of liquidity.

This can act as a cushion during tumultuous times and give you the ability to seize opportunities when they present themselves.

8. Risk reduction: Determine potential risks that might have an impact on your company and take steps to reduce them.

Create backup plans to address these risks.

9. Maintain open lines of communication with all relevant parties, such as staff members, investors, and clients, as the market becomes volatile. Transparency fosters trust.

10. Make sure your leadership team is on board with your vision and strategies for surviving market turbulence. During trying times, effective teamwork is essential.

11. Innovation: Look for novel ways to satisfy shifting customer needs and outperform rivals. This could entail digital transformation, process improvement, or product development.

12. Maintain a long-term perspective while addressing the immediate problems.

Opportunities for growth and the expansion of market share can arise in turbulent markets.

13. Connect with peers in your industry and business leaders to gain perspectives on how others are dealing with similar issues.

A natural component of the business cycle is market volatility, so keep that in mind. Successful CEOs are flexible, seize opportunities in the face of uncertainty, and set up their businesses for long-term success.

Even in challenging circumstances, it's crucial to maintain your resiliency, adaptability, and strategic focus.

Growth And Innovation.

As CEOs work to steer their organizations toward success and competitiveness, innovation and growth are frequently key objectives. CEOs can promote innovation and growth in the following ways.

1. Foster an Innovation Culture: CEOs can work to create an environment that rewards innovation, taking calculated risks, and trying new things. This includes honoring and rewarding creative projects and ideas.

2. Establish a vision for innovation that is consistent with the objectives and core values of the organization.

3. Allocate funds to research and development projects to investigate novel concepts, technologies, and product/service improvements.

4. Embrace Technology: Keep up with new developments and think about how you can use technology to enhance your offerings, procedures, and client experiences.

5. Customer-Centric Innovation: Recognize opportunities for innovation that meet the needs and pain points of customers by listening to their feedback and insights.

6. Cross-functional collaboration is encouraged to bring a variety of viewpoints and expertise to the innovation process.

7. Open innovation: Join forces with outside businesses, start-ups, or academic institutions to gain access to fresh concepts and technological advancements.

8. Acquisitions and Mergers: To accelerate growth, strategically buy out or combine with businesses that provide complementary technologies or capabilities.

9. Implement agile and lean methodologies to improve workflow, cut waste, and hasten the time it takes to market goods and services.

10. Risk Management: CEOs should effectively manage associated risks while fostering innovation, taking into account the potential effects on the organization.

11. Talent development: Invest in programs that help employees advance their skills so that there is a workforce that can effectively drive innovation.

12. Establish metrics and key performance indicators (KPIs) to monitor the development and effectiveness of innovation initiatives.

13. Examine potential avenues for market expansion, whether it be through geographic extension or industry diversification.

14. Customer Retention: Prioritize keeping current customers by providing excellent customer service and high-quality products while pursuing new customer acquisition strategies.

15. Sustainability and social responsibility: Take into account how innovation can be in line with sustainability objectives and social responsibility programs, which can also appeal to ethical consumers.

16. Encourage a culture of continuous improvement throughout the entire organization by fostering an atmosphere where small, incremental innovations are valued.

CEOs who are successful at fostering innovation and growth frequently strike a balance between taking advantage of new opportunities and risk management. They place a high priority on innovation as a strategic imperative because they realize how important it can be for long-term success and competitiveness in the fast-paced business environment of today.

Chapter 4

Creating A Positive Workplace Environment.

For employees' success and well-being as well as that of the organization as a whole, it is crucial to foster a positive work environment.

You are essential in establishing and preserving this positive environment in your capacity as CEO. The ways of doing this are:

1. Lead by example by exemplifying the attitudes and conduct you want to see in your company. Your behavior establishes the tone for the entire organization.

2. Foster open and honest communication throughout the organization by following the principle of clarity.

Share your thoughts, worries, and feedback with the staff.

3. Give your staff autonomy and decision-making power when it's appropriate to empower them.
Morale and drive may increase as a result.
4. Recognize and value the contributions that your staff members have made.
Recognize their efforts and accomplishments regularly.
5. Encourage a healthy work-life balance by establishing reasonable expectations and encouraging flexibility when it is possible.
6. Professional advancement: Invest in the education and training of your staff.
Give people the chance to advance their careers and receive mentoring and training.
7. Promote an inclusive and diverse workplace where each employee feels valued and welcomed.
More innovation and creativity follow from this.
8. Resolution of Conflicts: Resolve disputes quickly and productively.
To resolve conflicts and keep a positive work environment, provide resources and support.

9. Prioritize your employees' emotional and physical well-being.

Safety comes second.

As well as providing support for mental health, make sure safety precautions are in place.

10. Promote team-building exercises and opportunities for employees to interact and work together outside of the scope of their regular responsibilities.

11. Verify that your company's values and your employees' values are in line with each other.

The sense of purpose and meaning at work can be increased by a values-driven culture.

12. Establish mechanisms for employees to offer feedback and suggestions for improvement.

When appropriate, take action on this advice.

13. Celebrating Success: As a team, commemorate landmarks, triumphs, and accomplishments.

This supports a happy and motivated work environment.

14. Flexibility and adaptability: Be willing to change and adjust to circumstances and needs as they change. A flexible approach can make workers feel supported.

15. Conflict Resolution: Resolve disputes quickly and productively.
Offer tools and assistance for resolving conflicts and preserving a peaceful workplace.

It's important to keep in mind that creating a positive work environment takes dedication and consistency over time. In addition to increasing employee satisfaction and output, it also makes it easier to find and keep top talent, which ultimately helps the organization succeed.
As a CEO, supporting D&I initiatives is not only morally right but also advantageous for your company strategically.
To support D&I, follow these steps:

1. Show your commitment to D&I by using the phrase "Commitment from the Top.". Make it clear that diversity and inclusion are essential to the company's values and success, not just HR initiatives.
2. Set Clear Goals: Decide on quantifiable objectives and key performance indicators (KPIs) for diversity and inclusion.

Keep an eye on things and make the leadership responsible.

3. Make sure there is diversity at the executive and leadership levels.

Diverse leadership teams can promote more inclusive decision-making.

4. Review and update company policies to get rid of prejudice and discrimination.

Think about accommodating policies and flexible work schedules to promote inclusion.

5. Implement education and training programs to encourage inclusive behavior among staff members of all ranks and to increase awareness of unconscious bias.

6. Implement blind hiring procedures, expand your talent pool, and collaborate with groups that assist underrepresented groups.

7. Encourage the creation of employee resource groups (ERGs) that offer support and networking opportunities for diverse employees.

8. Expand supplier diversity initiatives to help minority-owned businesses and promote economic inclusion.

9. Share D&I challenges and progress with stakeholders, including staff members.
Accountability and trust are enhanced by transparency.
10. Foster an inclusive culture where everyone feels valued and respected and where all voices are heard. Immediately address discrimination and microaggressions.
11. Implement mentoring and sponsorship programs to aid underrepresented employees in advancing their careers.
12. In order to ensure pay equity across gender, race, and other demographics, compensation practices should be routinely reviewed.
13. Participate in neighborhood associations and groups that promote inclusion and diversity. Encourage your staff to volunteer and take part.
14. Data collection is important for determining areas for improvement and gauging the success of your D&I initiatives.
15. D&I efforts should be ongoing.
Continuous Improvement to reflect changing needs and objectives, regularly evaluate and modify your strategies.

By giving diversity and inclusion initiatives top priority, you not only improve workplace equity but also access a wider range of viewpoints and skills, which can foster innovation and enhance business results.

Projects promoting diversity and inclusion.

Leading diversity and inclusion (D&I) initiatives is undoubtedly a crucial responsibility for a CEO.

The steps you can take to promote diversity and inclusion in your company are broken down in more detail below:

1. Personal Commitment: Begin by stating your dedication to D&I on a personal level.
Tell us why it matters to you and the company.
2. Develop a D&I strategy that details your organization's objectives, plans, and milestones for advancing diversity and inclusion.
3. Make sure that your executive team is actively engaged in D&I initiatives and is in line with the strategy.
4. The goal should be to have a diverse board of directors. The organization as a whole may change as a result of diverse viewpoints at this level.
5. Implement recurring training programs on diversity and inclusion for staff members at all levels.

Pay attention to issues like cultural competency and unconscious bias.

6. Diverse Recruitment: Review your hiring and recruitment procedures.

Employ tactics to draw in a diverse pool of candidates, such as inclusive job descriptions and blind recruitment.

7. To eliminate prejudices and advance inclusivity in areas like hiring, advancement, and compensation, review and update the company's inclusive policies.

8. Encourage and support the creation of employee resource groups (ERGs) for different affinity groups within your organization.

9. Mentorship and sponsorship programs should be established to connect workers from underrepresented groups with influential individuals who can help them advance their careers.

10. Pay Equity: Regularly assess and close any racial or gender pay gaps in your company.

11. Establish definite accountability for D&I goals, and consider D&I metrics when evaluating managers' and leaders' job performance.

12. Transparency: Inform your stakeholders, including your staff, of data and progress on D&I initiatives.

Trust and accountability are enhanced by transparency.

13. Supplier Diversity: Support supplier diversity by buying goods and services from companies run by members of underrepresented groups.

14. Engage your community by collaborating with groups and projects that promote inclusion and diversity there.

15. Continuous Learning: Stay up to date on D&I best practices by continuing your education and joining D&I networks.

16. Listen and Act: Actively solicit feedback from staff members regarding their experiences and recommendations for improvement.

Establish systems that will allow workers to report instances of bias or discrimination.

17. Legal Compliance: Assure adherence to pertinent anti-discrimination and diversity laws.

18. To acknowledge progress and spur additional action, recognize diversity and inclusion accomplishments within your organization.

19. Recognize that D&I is a journey, not a one-time project, and make a long-term commitment to evaluate and modify your strategies regularly.

20. External Partnerships: Consider partnering with outside organizations and projects that advance diversity and inclusion (D&I) as well as joining trade associations that support these issues.

You can foster an environment where all employees feel valued, included, and empowered to give their best effort by actively leading and promoting D&I initiatives.

This will ultimately spur innovation and success for your company.

Chapter 5

The CEO's Private Life.

As a CEO navigates the difficulties and responsibilities of their leadership role, their inner world is a complex and dynamic landscape that includes their thoughts, feelings, and past experiences.

The following are a few significant elements of a CEO's inner world.

1. CEOs frequently shoulder a heavy load of duties, which can result in high levels of stress and pressure.

Managing this stress is an ongoing concern.

2. CEOs must make a variety of decisions every day, from strategic options to operational specifics. They struggle a lot with the results of their choices and the trade-offs they entail.

3. The CEO position can be lonely because they may have few peers within the company with whom they can openly discuss certain issues and choices.

4. CEOs must project decisiveness and confidence, but they may also occasionally feel uncertain or self-conscious about their decisions.

5. Balance: Struggling to maintain a healthy balance between work and personal obligations. CEOs might wonder if they are spending enough time on their families and personal needs.

6. To ensure alignment with their objectives and core values, CEOs constantly reflect on the long-term vision and strategy for their business.

7. Resilience: It's important to have the capacity to overcome obstacles and setbacks. CEOs frequently rely on their innate fortitude to keep going when things are tough.

8. CEOs may face moral and ethical conundrums in their decision-making, questioning the proper course of action in challenging circumstances.

9. Legacy and Impact: It's common for people to reflect on the legacy they want to leave behind and the impact they want to have on the organization and society.

10. The desire for personal development is constant. This is known as continuous learning. CEOs frequently look for opportunities to grow as leaders.

11. The inner world of a CEO is propelled by an intrinsic desire to lead and make a difference.

12. The development and maintenance of relationships with stakeholders, board members, and staff is a constant consideration.

13. As they navigate shifting market conditions and business challenges, CEOs must be flexible and open to change.

14. Crisis management: A crucial component of a CEO's inner world is mentally and emotionally preparing for handling crises.

15. The maintenance of one's physical and mental well-being is essential. CEOs may struggle to prioritize self-care amidst their busy schedules.

The unique requirements and responsibilities of the CEO's leadership role have shaped their inner world, which is a dynamic and introspective space.

Resilience, self-awareness, and a dedication to lifelong learning and development are prerequisites.

Impact And Legacy.

The contributions and long-lasting effects a CEO has while serving in a leadership capacity are referred to as their legacy and impact.

The organization's employees, stakeholders, and the larger community can all be impacted by the CEO's actions and decisions.

A CEO's legacy and impact can be summarized as follows:

1. Organizational Growth: A CEO's strategic vision and leadership can significantly increase sales, market share, and profitability, making a long-lasting impact on the company's success.

2. CEOs have a cultural influence because they set the standards for behaviors, expectations, and values within their organizations.

Even after they leave, a good culture can persist.

3. Innovation and Organizational Transformation: CEOs who support innovation and drive organizational transformations can position their businesses as market leaders and leave a legacy of adaptability and advancement.

4. Talent development: A CEO's investment in leadership pipelines and talent development can leave a legacy of future leaders who will lead the company forward.

5. Corporate social responsibility initiatives can have a positive effect on communities, the environment, and social causes when CEOs give them top priority.

6. A CEO's ethical leadership and dedication to quality can improve the company's reputation, which can last even after they leave the position.

7. Financial stewardship: An organization's legacy of financial sustainability and stability can be created by responsible financial management.

8. Diversity and inclusion: A CEO's initiatives to advance diversity and inclusion can foster a more accepting workplace culture that lasts after their departure.

9. Industry Influence: A few CEOs go on to become thought leaders in their fields, influencing the direction of their industries and having a

long-lasting effect on how things are done in those fields.

10. Customer Loyalty: CEOs who put customers' needs first can create a legacy of loyal patrons and a devoted following for their brands.

11. Institutional Memory: A CEO's strategic choices and overall direction help shape the organization's institutional memory and long-term course.

12. Philanthropy: CEOs who support philanthropic endeavors and causes can have a positive impact on society and motivate employees to make similar contributions.

13. Effective CEO succession planning guarantees a seamless changeover and ongoing leadership, protecting the CEO's legacy.

The leadership style, priorities, and values of a CEO have a significant impact on their legacy. Successful CEOs frequently work to leave a legacy that goes beyond short-term financial gains and concentrates on generating long-term value for the company, its stakeholders, and society at large.

Your decisions and actions as the CEO (Chief Executive Officer) of a business or organization have the potential to make a big difference and leave a lasting impression. Examining impact and legacies in the context of a CEO, let's see how they work.

Impact.

1. Financial Impact: The CEO is in charge of the business's finances. The financial performance of the business is directly impacted by your decisions regarding investments, cost control, revenue generation, and profitability. A favorable impact could raise the value of the company's stock, whereas a negative impact might cause financial instability.

2. Market Impact: CEOs have a say in how a company is positioned in the marketplace. The market share and reputation of the company can be shaped by strategies for market expansion, product development, and competition.

3. Impact on Employees: CEOs are extremely important in determining the corporate culture and employee morale. While poor leadership can have the opposite effect, good leadership can result in a motivated workforce, high retention rates, and increased productivity.

4. The social and environmental impact of a company is something that many contemporary CEOs are expected to take into account. A positive influence on society and the environment can be achieved through sustainable practices, corporate social responsibility (CSR) programs, and ethical decision-making.

Legacies:

1. Product Development and Innovation: CEOs who place a high priority on the creation of ground-breaking goods or services leave a legacy of technological advancement. Under the direction of Steve Jobs at Apple, this may have included the launch of revolutionary products like the iPhone.

2. Cultural Legacy: The corporate culture and values of the company can be shaped by the CEO. A CEO can leave a cultural legacy that endures long after their tenure if they promote an inclusive, diverse, and ethical culture.

3. Leadership Style: The leadership techniques used by your successors as well as the performance of the company under your direction can be influenced by your leadership style. Future CEOs may be inspired by a legacy of successful leadership.

4. Strategic Vision: CEOs who establish a compelling and distinct strategic vision for their organization leave a legacy of direction.Even after the CEO has stepped down from their position, this vision can still steer the business for years.

5. Philanthropy and social responsibility: CEOs who support charitable causes and community service initiatives can leave a lasting legacy. This covers programs for addressing poverty, providing healthcare, and more.

6. Financial Stewardship: CEOs who effectively oversee the business's finances and guarantee its long-term stability and growth leave a legacy of sound financial management that benefits stakeholders and shareholders.

It's critical to remember that a CEO's influence and legacy are not only evaluated financially but also in terms of their impact on the culture, values, and contributions they make to society. CEOs have a special opportunity to influence their companies' futures and make a significant contribution to both business and society.

Conclusion.

The importance of leadership, adaptability, and perseverance becomes undeniably profound in the complex role of a CEO. As we come to a close with our reflections, it is clear that these characteristics form the basis of successful leadership at the highest levels of business.

The essence of the CEO is defined by leadership, the art of motivating and directing an organization toward a common vision. It serves as a guiding light, inspiring groups of people to work together toward common objectives.

The CEO's secret weapon against obsolescence is adaptability, or the ability to change course in a rapidly changing environment.

An organization's relevance and resilience are ensured by its capacity to reevaluate strategies and embrace innovation.

But what distinguishes outstanding CEOs is their capacity for perseverance.

They continue moving forward despite significant obstacles and setbacks thanks to their unwavering resolve.

What makes good CEOs great is their ability to weather challenges and persevere in the face of adversity.

As we draw to a close, keep in mind that qualities like perseverance, leadership, and adaptability must be continually developed. They serve as the foundation for a CEO's personality and influence not only the future of their company but also the direction of the sector as a whole.

These qualities serve as the compass, the lifeline, and the driving force in the never-ending journey of leadership.

In conclusion, let it be known that those who aspire to or already hold the position of CEO will be judged on their ability to adapt during difficult times and their unwavering perseverance through the most trying of tribulations.

May these qualities serve as your compass as you navigate the complicated business world, pointing you in the direction of transformative success and a lasting legacy.